MARKET FRESH QUILTS

Nature's bounty of fresh vegetables, fruits, and flowers is celebrated in these beautiful quilts by Tammy Tadd. The rich, vivid colors of an autumn harvest are reproduced using fat quarters in "My Big Fat Quarter Quilt." A smaller version, "My Little Fat Quarter Quilt," displays the gorgeous colors of spring flowers. "Peaches and Cream" and "Snappin' Green Beans" invoke memories of long summer days preparing and feasting on homegrown delicacies. Choose from these four lovely designs, and celebrate the beauty of nature with your own "market fresh" quilt.

Meet the Designer

Tammy Tadd is blessed with a family whose support and encouragement inspire her to create dozens of original quilts.

"It was my mother," Tammy says, "who never let me feel that anything was beyond my capability."

"Mom and I have always done well at hand work, including sewing, painting, and crafting." Tammy says. "Mom has quilted for more than 20 years."

This "we can do it" attitude goes back another generation to Tammy's Grandma Bessie, who taught it to Tammy's mother.

"When Mom and I decided to market our quilting patterns, our first designs were called 'The Grandma Bessie Series.' Grandma went to be with the Lord several years ago, but she is still close to our hearts. Other pattern themes we have done are our regular Tammy Tadd Designs, Sunday Sampler Series, and Taddpoles Children's Series."

With five children of her own, Tammy finds that creating quilt patterns allows her to be a full-time mom. Gary, her husband, assists by designing pattern packages.

LEISURE ARTS, INC.
Little Rock, Arkansas

SNAPPIN' Green Beans

Quilt made by Velda Grubbs.

Quilt Size: 85" x 94" (216 cm x 239 cm)
Block Size: 9" x 9" (23 cm x 23 cm)

YARDAGE REQUIREMENTS

Yardage is based on 43"/44" (109 cm/112 cm) wide fabric.
- $4^3/_4$ yds (4.3 m) of white-on-white print fabric
- $3^3/_4$ yds (3.4 m) of light green print fabric
- $2^7/_8$ yds (2.6 m) of medium green print fabric
- $^3/_4$ yd (69 cm) of dark green print fabric
- $1^1/_4$ yds (1.1 m) of navy print fabric
- $7^7/_8$ yds (7.2 m) of fabric for backing
- 1 yd (91 cm) of fabric for binding

You will also need:
- 93" x 102" (236 cm x 259 cm) piece of batting

CUTTING OUT THE PIECES

Measurements include $^1/_4$" seam allowances. Follow **Template Cutting**, *page 35, to make templates from patterns* **A** *and* **B** *on page 7. Follow* **Rotary Cutting**, *page 34, to cut fabric.*

From white-on-white print fabric:
- Cut 10 **strips** 2"w.
- Cut 9 strips $3^7/_8$"w. From these strips, cut 84 **large squares** $3^7/_8$" x $3^7/_8$".
- Cut 9 strips 2"w. From these strips, cut 176 **smallest squares** 2" x 2".
- Cut 1 strip 2"w. From this strip, cut 8 **small rectangles** 2" x $3^1/_2$".
- Cut 5 strips $3^7/_8$"w. From these strips, cut 42 squares $3^7/_8$" x $3^7/_8$". Cut squares *once* diagonally to make 84 **large triangles**.
- Cut 6 strips $2^3/_8$"w. From these strips, cut 84 squares $2^3/_8$" x $2^3/_8$". Cut squares *once* diagonally to make 168 **small triangles**.
- Cut 106 **A's** from template.
- Cut 4 **B's** and 4 **B's in reverse** from template.

From light green print fabric:
- Cut 8 **strips** 2"w.
- Cut 5 strips $3^7/_8$"w. From these strips, cut 42 **large squares** $3^7/_8$" x $3^7/_8$".
- Cut 3 strips $2^3/_8$"w. From these strips, cut 42 **small squares** $2^3/_8$" x $2^3/_8$".
- Cut 8 strips 2"w. From these strips, cut 84 **small rectangles** 2" x $3^1/_2$".
- Cut 8 strips $3^1/_2$"w. From these strips, cut 47 **large rectangles** $3^1/_2$" x $6^1/_2$".
- Cut 3 strips $3^7/_8$"w. From these strips, cut 21 squares $3^7/_8$" x $3^7/_8$". Cut squares *once* diagonally to make 42 **large triangles**.
- Cut 55 **A's** from template.

From medium green print fabric:
- Cut 5 strips $3^7/_8$"w. From these strips, cut 42 **large squares** $3^7/_8$" x $3^7/_8$".
- Cut 2 strips $3^1/_2$"w. From these strips, cut 21 **medium squares** $3^1/_2$" x $3^1/_2$".
- Cut 1 strip 2"w. From this strip, cut 8 **smallest squares** 2" x 2".
- Cut 8 strips $3^1/_2$"w. From these strips, cut 47 **large rectangles** $3^1/_2$" x $6^1/_2$".
- Cut 3 strips $3^7/_8$"w. From these strips, cut 21 squares $3^7/_8$" x $3^7/_8$". Cut squares *once* diagonally to make 42 **large triangles**.
- Cut 55 **A's** from template.

From dark green print fabric:
- Cut 3 strips $2^3/_8$"w. From these strips, cut 42 **small squares** $2^3/_8$" x $2^3/_8$".
- Cut 6 strips $2^3/_8$"w. From these strips, cut 84 squares $2^3/_8$" x $2^3/_8$". Cut squares *once* diagonally to make 168 **small triangles**.

From navy print fabric:
- Cut 18 **strips** 2"w.
- Cut 2 strips $3^1/_2$"w. From these strips, cut 12 **medium squares** $3^1/_2$" x $3^1/_2$".

MAKING THE BLOCKS

*Use ¼" seam allowances throughout. Follow **Piecing**, page 35, and **Pressing**, page 36, to make **Blocks**.*

1. Draw diagonal line (corner to corner) on wrong side of each white **large square**. With right sides together, place 1 white **large square** on top of 1 medium green **large square**. Stitch seam ¼" from each side of drawn line (**Fig. 1**).

   Fig. 1

   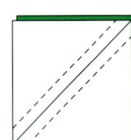

2. Cut along drawn line and press open to make 2 **Triangle-Square A's**. Make 84 **Triangle-Square A's**.

   Triangle-Square A's (make 84)

3. Repeat Steps 1 and 2 using white **large squares** and light green **large squares** to make 84 **Triangle-Square B's**.

   Triangle-Square B's (make 84)

    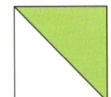

4. Sew 1 **Triangle-Square A** and 2 **Triangle-Square B's** together to make **Unit 1**. Make 42 **Unit 1's**.

   Unit 1 (make 42)

   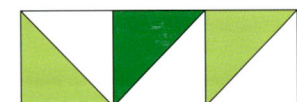

5. Sew 2 **Triangle-Square A's** and 1 medium green **medium square** together to make **Unit 2**. Make 21 **Unit 2's**.

   Unit 2 (make 21)

6. Sew 2 **Unit 1's** and 1 **Unit 2** together to make **Block A**. Make 21 **Block A's**.

   Block A (make 21)

7. Sew 2 medium green **large triangles** and 2 light green **large triangles** together to make **Unit 3**. Make 21 **Unit 3's**.

   Unit 3 (make 21)

   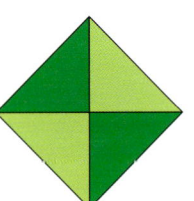

8. Draw diagonal line (corner to corner) on wrong side of each light green **small square**. With right sides together, place 1 light green **small square** on top of 1 dark green **small square**. Stitch seam ¹/₄" from each side of drawn line (**Fig. 2**).

Fig. 2

9. Cut along drawn line and press open to make 2 **Triangle-Square C's**. Make 84 **Triangle-Square C's**.

Triangle-Square C's (make 84)

10. Sew 1 **Triangle-Square C** and 2 white **small triangles** together to make **Unit 4**. Make 84 **Unit 4's**.

Unit 4 (make 84)

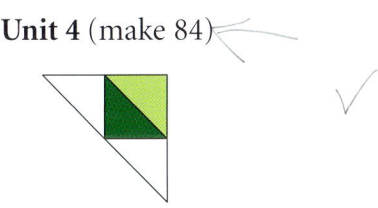

11. Sew 1 **Unit 3** and 4 **Unit 4's** together to make **Unit 5**. Make 21 **Unit 5's**.

Unit 5 (make 21)

12. With right sides together, place 1 white **smallest square** on one end of 1 light green **small rectangle** and stitch diagonally (**Fig. 3**). Trim ¹/₄" from stitching line (**Fig. 4**). Open up and press, pressing seam allowances to darker fabric (**Fig. 5**).

Fig. 3

Fig. 4

Fig. 5

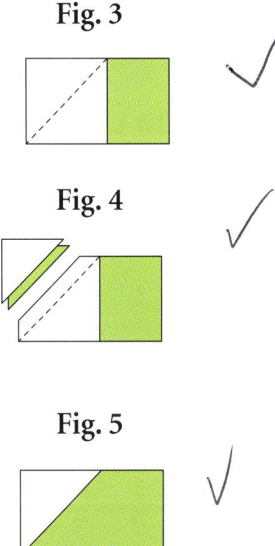

13. Place another white **smallest square** on opposite end of **small rectangle**. Stitch and trim as shown in **Fig. 6**. Open up and press to complete **Flying Geese Unit**. Make 84 **Flying Geese Units**.

Fig. 6

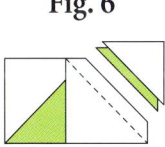

Flying Geese Unit (make 84)

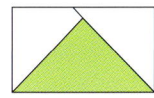

14. Sew 1 **Flying Geese Unit** and 2 dark green **small triangles** together to make **Unit 6**. Make 84 **Unit 6's**.

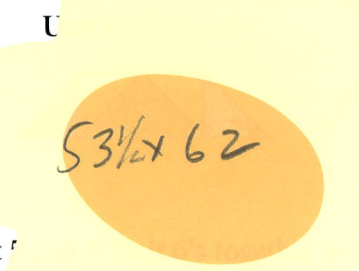

53½ x 62

15. Sew 1 Unit ... Unit 7. Ma...

16. Sew 1 **Unit 7** and 4 white **large triangles** together to make **Block B**. Make 21 **Block B's**.

Block B (make 21)

MAKING THE BORDERS

Use $1/4$" seam allowances throughout. Refer to **Quilt Top Diagram**, page 8, and photo, page 9, for placement.

1. Sew 2 navy **strips** together to make 1 long strip 2"w. Make 4 long strips. Trim 2 long strips to 2" x $63^{1}/_{2}$" for **side first (inner) borders**. Trim remaining long strips to 2" x $57^{1}/_{2}$" for **top/bottom (inner) first border**.
2. Sew 2 light green **strips** together to make 1 long strip 2"w. Make 4 long strips. Trim 2 long strips to 2" x $66^{1}/_{2}$" for **side second borders**. Trim remaining long strips to 2" x $60^{1}/_{2}$" for **top/bottom second borders**.
3. Sew 1 white **strip** and 1 navy **strip** together to make **Strip Set A**. Make 10 **Strip Set A's**. Cut across **Strip Set A's** at 2" intervals to make 180 **Unit 8's**.

Strip Set A (make 10)   **Unit 8** (make 180)

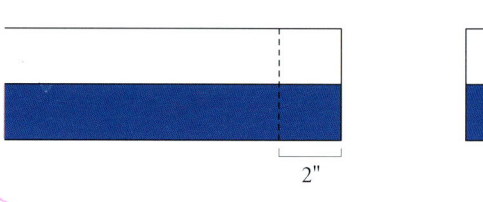

4. Alternating colors, sew 46 **Unit 8's** together to make **side third border**. Make 2 **side third borders**.
5. Alternating colors, sew 44 **Unit 8's** together to make **top third border**. Repeat to make **bottom third border**.
6. Sew 1 white **smallest square** and 1 medium green **smallest square** together to make **Unit 9**. Make 8 **Unit 9's**.

Unit 9 (make 8)

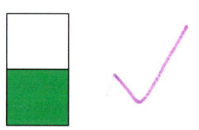

7. Sew 1 **Unit 9** and 1 white **small rectangle** together to make **Unit 10**. Make 8 **Unit 10's**.

Unit 10 (make 8)

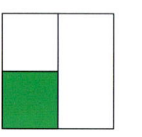 

8. Sew 2 **Unit 10's** and 2 navy **medium squares** together to make **Border Block**. Make 4 **Border Blocks**.

Border Block (make 4)

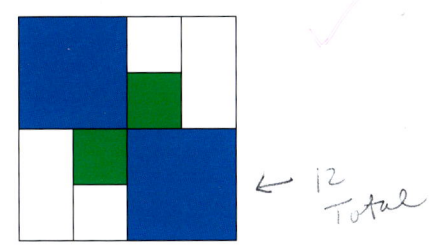

← 12 Total

9. Beginning with light green and alternating colors, sew 13 light green **large rectangles** and 12 medium green **large rectangles** together to make **left side fourth border**.
10. Beginning with medium green and alternating colors, sew 13 medium green **large rectangles** and 12 light green **large rectangles** together to make **right side fourth border**.
11. Alternating colors, sew 11 medium green **large rectangles** and 11 light green **large rectangles** together; sew 1 **Border Block** to each end to make **top fourth border**.
12. Alternating colors, sew 11 medium green **large rectangles** and 11 light green **large rectangles** together; sew 1 **Border Block** to each end to make **bottom fourth border**.
13. Sew 28 white **A's**, 15 light green **A's**, and 14 medium green **A's** together; sew 1 white **B** to one end and 1 white **B in reverse** to other end to make **left side fifth (outer) border**.
14. Sew 28 white **A's**, 15 medium green **A's**, and 14 light green **A's** together; sew 1 white **B** to one end and 1 white **B in reverse** to other end to make **right side fifth border**.
15. Sew 25 white **A's**, 13 light green **A's**, and 13 medium green **A's** together; sew 1 white **B** and 1 navy **medium square** to one end, and 1 white **B in reverse** and 1 navy **medium square** to other end to make **top fifth border**.
16. Sew 25 white **A's**, 13 light green **A's**, and 13 medium green **A's** together; sew 1 white **B** and 1 navy **medium square** to one end, and 1 white **B in reverse** and 1 navy **medium square** to other end to make **bottom fifth border**.

ASSEMBLING THE QUILT TOP

*Use ¹/₄" seam allowances throughout. For all borders, match centers and corners and ease in any fullness. Refer to **Quilt Top Diagram**, page 8, and photo, page 9, for placement.*

1. Sew 3 **Block A's** and 3 **Block B's** together to make **Row**. Make 7 **Rows**.
2. Sew **Rows** together to complete center section of quilt top.
3. Add **side, top, then bottom first borders** to quilt top. Repeat to add **second, third, fourth**, and **fifth borders**.

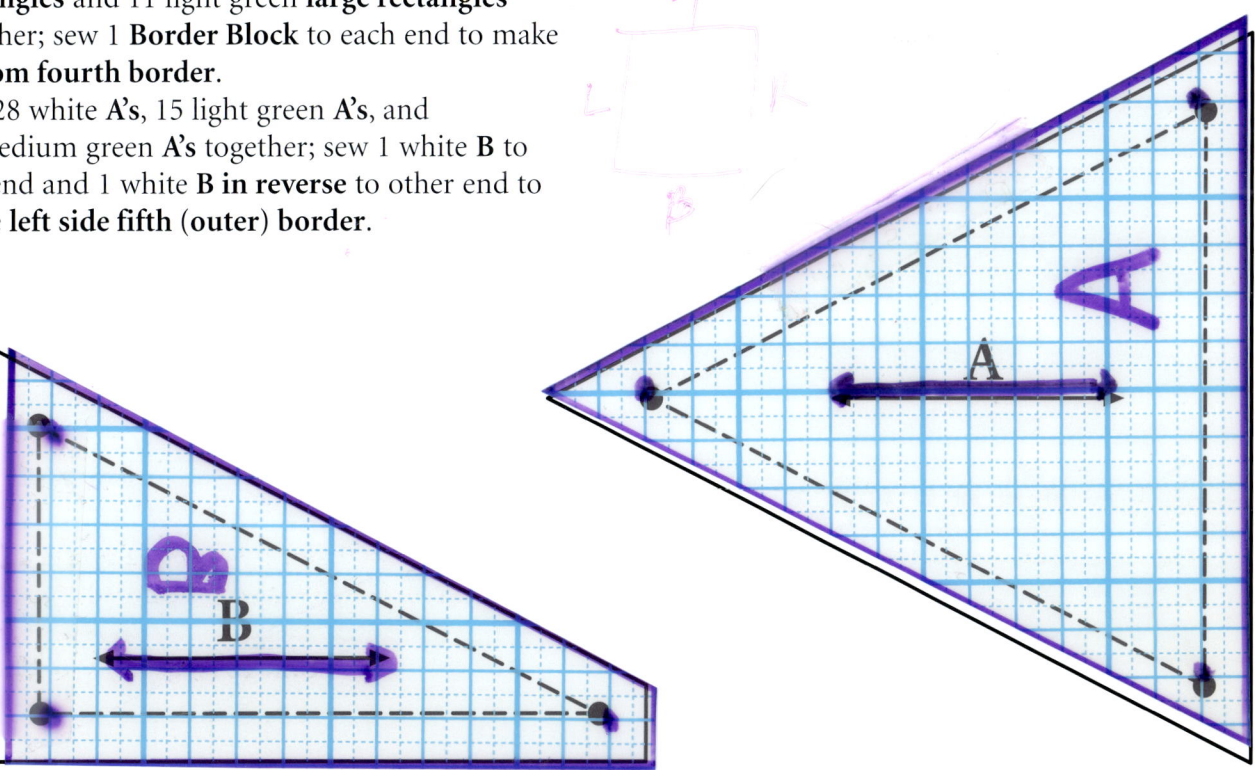

COMPLETING THE QUILT

1. Follow **Quilting**, page 36, to mark, layer, and quilt as desired. Our quilt is machine quilted.
2. Cut a 32" square of binding fabric. Follow **Binding**, page 40, to bind quilt using 2½"w bias binding with mitered corners.

Quilt Top Diagram

PEACHES & Cream

Quilt made by Velda Grubbs.

Quilt Size: 48" x 57" (122 cm x 145 cm)
Block Size: 9" x 9" (23 cm x 23 cm)

YARDAGE REQUIREMENTS

Yardage is based on 43"/44" (109 cm/112 cm) wide fabric.

- ⁵/₈ yd (57 cm) of green solid fabric
- ¹/₄ yd (23 cm) of green print fabric
- ⁵/₈ yd (57 cm) of purple solid fabric
- ¹/₄ yd (23 cm) of purple print fabric
- ⁵/₈ yd (57 cm) of peach solid fabric
- ¹/₄ yd (23 cm) of peach print fabric
- ³/₄ yd (69 cm) of cream solid fabric
- ¹/₂ yd (46 cm) of cream print fabric
- 1¹/₄ yds (1.1 m) of multi-color plaid fabric (includes binding)
- 1³/₈ yds (1.3 m) of multi-color large print fabric
- 3⁵/₈ yds (3.3 m) of fabric for backing

You will also need:
   56" x 65" (142 cm x 165 cm) piece of batting

CUTTING OUT THE PIECES

*Measurements include ¹/₄" seam allowances. Borders include an extra 2" in length and will be trimmed after quilt top center is complete. Follow **Rotary Cutting**, page 34, to cut fabric.*

From green solid fabric:
- Cut 2 strips 3¹/₂"w. From these strips, cut 16 **large squares** 3¹/₂" x 3¹/₂".
- Cut 1 strip 2¹/₂"w. From this strip, cut 6 **medium squares** 2¹/₂" x 2¹/₂".
- Cut 4 strips 2"w. From these strips, cut 64 **small squares** 2" x 2".

From green print fabric:
- Cut 4 strips 2"w. From these strips, cut 64 **small squares** 2" x 2".

From purple solid fabric:
- Cut 2 strips 3¹/₂"w. From these strips, cut 16 **large squares** 3¹/₂" x 3¹/₂".
- Cut 1 strip 2¹/₂"w. From this strip, cut 5 **medium squares** 2¹/₂" x 2¹/₂".
- Cut 4 strips 2"w. From these strips, cut 64 **small squares** 2" x 2".

From purple print fabric:
- Cut 4 strips 2"w. From these strips, cut 64 **small squares** 2" x 2".

From peach solid fabric:
- Cut 2 strips 3¹/₂"w. From these strips, cut 16 **large squares** 3¹/₂" x 3¹/₂".
- Cut 1 strip 2¹/₂"w. From this strip, cut 5 **medium squares** 2¹/₂" x 2¹/₂".
- Cut 4 strips 2"w. From these strips, cut 64 **small squares** 2" x 2".

From peach print fabric:
- Cut 4 strips 2"w. From these strips, cut 64 **small squares** 2" x 2".

From cream solid fabric:
- Cut 5 strips 3¹/₂"w. From these strips, cut 48 **large squares** 3¹/₂" x 3¹/₂".
- Cut 2 strips 2¹/₂"w. From these strips, cut 20 **medium squares** 2¹/₂" x 2¹/₂".

From cream print fabric:
- Cut 2 strips $3^{1}/_{2}$"w. From this strip, cut 16 **large squares** $3^{1}/_{2}$" x $3^{1}/_{2}$".
- Cut 2 **side inner borders** $1^{1}/_{2}$" x $38^{1}/_{2}$".
- Cut 2 **top/bottom inner borders** $1^{1}/_{2}$" x $31^{1}/_{2}$".

From multi-color plaid fabric:
- Cut 2 *lengthwise* **side middle borders** $3^{1}/_{2}$" x $40^{1}/_{2}$".
- Cut 2 *lengthwise* **top/bottom middle borders** $3^{1}/_{2}$" x $31^{1}/_{2}$".

Set aside remaining multi-color plaid fabric for binding.

From multi-color large print fabric:
- Cut 2 *lengthwise* **side outer borders** $6^{1}/_{2}$" x $46^{1}/_{2}$".
- Cut 2 *lengthwise* **top/bottom outer borders** $6^{1}/_{2}$" x $37^{1}/_{2}$".

MAKING THE BLOCKS

*Use $^{1}/_{4}$" seam allowances throughout. Follow **Piecing**, page 35, and **Pressing**, page 36, to make **Blocks**.*

1. With right sides together, place 1 purple print **small square** on 1 corner of 1 peach solid **large square** and stitch diagonally (**Fig. 1**). Trim $^{1}/_{4}$" from stitching line (**Fig. 2**). Open up and press, pressing seam allowances to darker fabric (**Fig. 3**).

Fig. 1

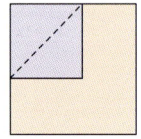

Fig. 2

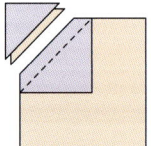

Fig. 3

2. Continue adding purple print **small squares** to corners of peach solid **large square** as shown in **Fig. 4**. Open up and press to complete **Unit 1**. Make 16 **Unit 1's**.

Fig. 4

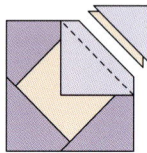

Unit 1 (make 16)

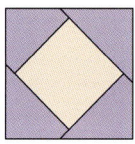

3. Repeat Steps 1 and 2 using green solid **small squares** and cream solid **large squares** to make 16 **Unit 2's**.

Unit 2 (make 16)

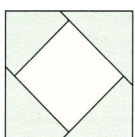

4. Sew 2 **Unit 1's** and 1 **Unit 2** together to make **Unit 3**. Make 8 **Unit 3's**.

Unit 3 (make 8)

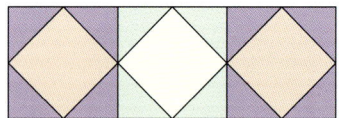

5. Sew 2 **Unit 2's** and 1 cream print **large square** together to make **Unit 4**. Make 4 **Unit 4's**.

Unit 4 (make 4)

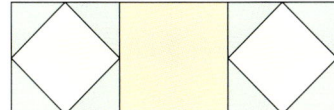

6. Sew 2 **Unit 3's** and 1 **Unit 4** together to make **Block A**. Make 4 **Block A's**.

Block A (make 4)

7. Repeat Steps 1 – 6 using peach print **small squares** and green solid **large squares** for **Unit 1's** and purple solid **small squares** and cream solid **large squares** for **Unit 2's** to make 4 **Block B's**.

Block B (make 4)

8. Repeat Steps 1 – 6 using green print **small squares** and purple solid **large squares** for **Unit 1's** and peach solid **small squares** and cream solid **large squares** for **Unit 2's** to make 4 **Block C's**.

Block C (make 4)

MAKING THE BORDER BLOCKS
Use ¼" seam allowances throughout.

1. Sew 2 cream solid **medium squares** and 1 peach solid medium square together to make **Unit 5**. Make 3 **Unit 5's**.

Unit 5 (make 3)

2. Sew 2 purple solid **medium squares** and 1 cream solid medium square together to make **Unit 6**.

Unit 6

3. Sew 2 cream solid **medium squares** and 1 green solid **medium square** together to make **Unit 7**. Make 2 **Unit 7's**.

Unit 7 (make 2)

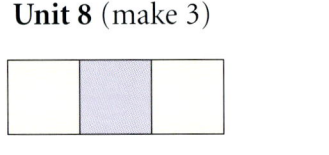

4. Sew 2 cream solid **medium squares** and 1 purple solid **medium square** together to make **Unit 8**. Make 3 **Unit 8's**.

Unit 8 (make 3)

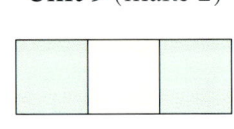

5. Sew 2 green solid **medium squares** and 1 cream solid **medium square** together to make **Unit 9**. Make 2 **Unit 9's**.

Unit 9 (make 2)

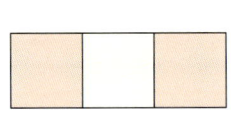

6. Sew 2 peach solid **medium squares** and 1 cream solid **medium square** together to make **Unit 10**.

Unit 10

7. Sew 1 **Unit 5**, 1 **Unit 6**, and 1 **Unit 7** together to make **Border Block A**.

Border Block A

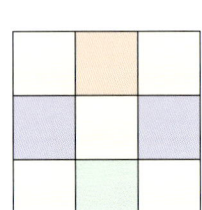

8. Sew 1 **Unit 8**, 1 **Unit 10**, and 1 **Unit 7** together to make **Border Block B**.

Border Block B

9. Sew 1 **Unit 8**, 1 **Unit 9**, and 1 **Unit 5** together to make **Border Block C**. Make 2 **Border Block C's**.

Border Block C (make 2)

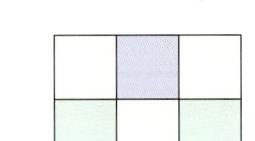

14

ASSEMBLING THE QUILT

*Use ¼" seam allowances throughout. Refer to **Quilt Top Diagram**, page 16, and photo, page 17, for placement.*

1. Sew 1 **Block A**, 1 **Block B**, and 1 **Block C** together to make **Row 1**. Make 2 **Row 1**'s.

Row 1 (make 2)

2. Sew 1 **Block C**, 1 **Block A**, and 1 **Block B** together to make **Row 2**.

Row 2

3. Sew 1 **Block B**, 1 **Block C**, and 1 **Block A** together to make **Row 3**.

Row 3

4. Sew 1 **Row 1**, **Row 2**, **Row 3**, then 1 **Row 1** together to complete center section of quilt top.
5. Measure *length* across center of center section of quilt top and trim **side inner borders** to determined length. Sew **side inner borders** to center section of quilt top.
6. Measure *width* across center of quilt top (including added borders) and trim **top/bottom inner borders** to determined length. Sew **top/bottom inner borders** to quilt top.
7. Measure *length* across center of quilt top, and trim **side middle borders** to determined length. Measure *width* across center of quilt top and trim **top/bottom middle borders** to determined length.
8. Sew 1 cream print **large square** to each end of **top** and **bottom middle borders**. Sew **side**, **top**, then **bottom middle borders** to quilt top.
9. Measure *length* across center of quilt top, and trim **side outer borders** to determined length. Measure *width* across center of quilt top and trim **top/bottom outer borders** to determined length.
10. Referring to **Quilt Top Diagram**, page 16, sew **Border Square A** to one end of **top outer border** and sew 1 **Border Square C** to the other end.
11. Sew 1 **Border Square C** to one end of **bottom outer border** and sew **Border Square B** to the other end.
12. Sew **side**, **top**, then **bottom outer borders** to quilt top.

COMPLETING THE QUILT

1. Follow **Quilting**, page 36, to mark, layer, and quilt as desired. Our quilt is machine quilted.

2. Cut a 25" square of binding fabric. Follow **Binding**, page 40, to bind quilt using $2^1/_2$"w bias binding with mitered corners.

Quilt Top Diagram

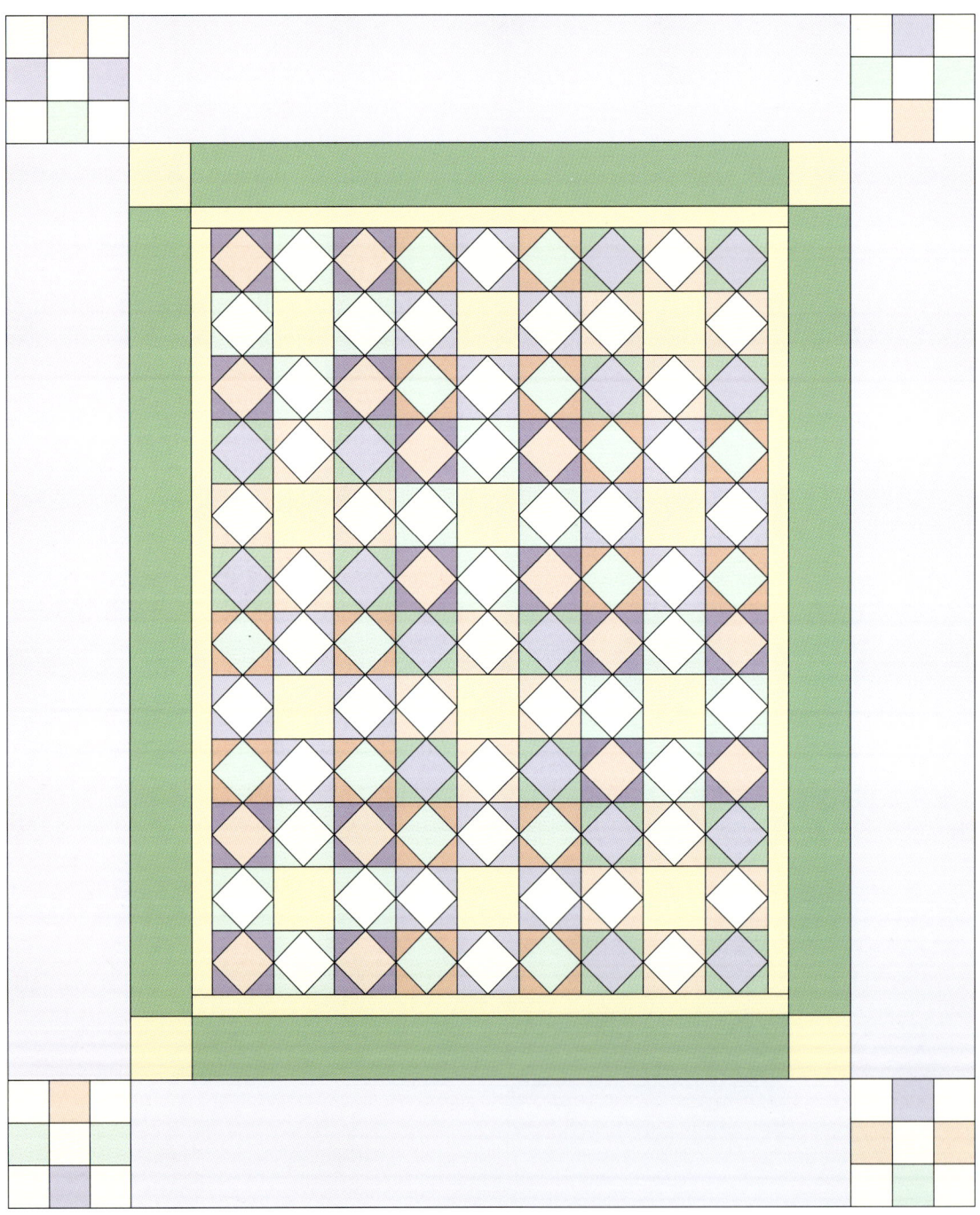

MY BIG Fat Quarter Quilt

Quilt made by Velda Grubbs and Dianna Olson.

Quilt Size: 87" x 103" (221 cm x 262 cm)
Block Size: 16" x 16" (41 cm x 41 cm)

YARDAGE REQUIREMENTS

Fat quarters measure approximately 18" x 22" (46 cm x 56 cm). The number of fat quarters we recommend is generous to allow for more variety in prints. Yardages are based on 43"/44" (109 cm/112 cm) wide fabric.

27 fat quarters of assorted tan print fabrics
13 fat quarters of assorted brown print fabrics
7 fat quarters of assorted green print fabrics
5 fat quarters of assorted red print fabrics
5 fat quarters of assorted blue print fabrics
$2^7/_8$ yds (2.6 m) of tan print fabric for borders
8 yds (7.3 m) of fabric for backing
1 yd (91 cm) of fabric for binding

You will also need:
95" x 111" (241 cm x 282 cm) piece of batting

CUTTING OUT THE PIECES

Measurements include $1/4$" seam allowances. Cutting lengths given for borders are exact. Follow **Rotary Cutting**, page 34, to cut fabric. Cut strips from fat quarters across 18" length.

From assorted tan print fabrics:
- Cut 64 strips $2^7/_8$"w. From these strips, cut 320 **squares** $2^7/_8$" x $2^7/_8$".
- Cut 208 **strips** $1^1/_2$"w.

From assorted brown print fabrics:
- Cut 64 strips $2^7/_8$"w. From these strips, cut 320 **squares** $2^7/_8$" x $2^7/_8$".
- Cut 20 **strips** $1^1/_2$"w.

From assorted green print fabrics:
- Cut 84 **strips** $1^1/_2$"w.

From assorted red print fabrics:
- Cut 52 **strips** $1^1/_2$"w.

From assorted blue print fabrics:
- Cut 52 **strips** $1^1/_2$"w.

From tan print fabric for borders:
- Cut 2 *lengthwise* **side outer borders** $3^1/_2$" x $96^1/_2$".
- Cut 2 *lengthwise* **top/bottom outer borders** $3^1/_2$" x $86^1/_2$".
- Cut 2 *lengthwise* **side inner borders** $4^1/_2$" x $80^1/_2$".
- Cut 2 *lengthwise* **top/bottom inner borders** $4^1/_2$" x $72^1/_2$".

MAKING THE BLOCKS

Use $1/4$" seam allowances throughout. Follow **Piecing**, page 35, and **Pressing**, page 36, to make **Blocks**.

1. Draw diagonal line (corner to corner) on wrong side of each tan **square**. With right sides together, place 1 tan **square** on top of 1 brown **square**. Stitch seam $1/4$" from each side of drawn line (**Fig. 1**).

Fig. 1

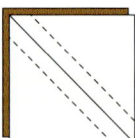

2. Cut along drawn line and press open to make 2 **Triangle-Squares**. Make 640 **Triangle-Squares**.

Triangle-Squares (make 640)

3. Sew 1 green **strip** and 1 tan **strip** together to make **Strip Set A**. Make 64 **Strip Set A's**. Cut across **Strip Set A's** at 1$^1/_2$" intervals to make **Unit 1**. Make 640 **Unit 1's**.

Strip Set A (make 64)   **Unit 1** (make 640)

4. Sew 1 red **strip** and 1 tan **strip** together to make **Strip Set B**. Make 32 **Strip Set B's**. Cut across **Strip Set B's** at 1$^1/_2$" intervals to make **Unit 2**. Make 320 **Unit 2's**.

Strip Set B (make 32)   **Unit 2** (make 320)

 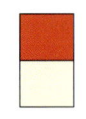

5. Sew 1 blue **strip** and 1 tan **strip** together to make **Strip Set C**. Make 32 **Strip Set C's**. Cut across **Strip Set C's** at 1$^1/_2$" intervals to make **Unit 3**. Make 320 **Unit 3's**.

Strip Set C (make 32)   **Unit 3** (make 320)

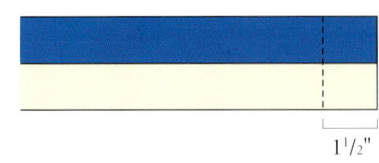 

6. Sew 2 **Unit 1's** together to make **Unit 4**. Make 320 **Unit 4's**.

Unit 4 (make 320)

7. Sew 2 **Unit 2's** together to make **Unit 5**. Make 160 **Unit 5's**.

Unit 5 (make 160)

8. Sew 2 **Unit 3's** together to make **Unit 6**. Make 160 **Unit 6's**.

Unit 6 (make 160)

9. Sew 2 **Unit 4's** and 2 **Triangle-Squares** together to make **Unit 7**. Make 160 **Unit 7's**.

Unit 7 (make 160)

10. Sew 2 **Unit 5's** and 2 **Triangle-Squares** together to make **Unit 8**. Make 80 **Unit 8's**.

Unit 8 (make 80)

11. Sew 2 **Unit 6's** and 2 **Triangle-Squares** together to make **Unit 9**. Make 80 **Unit 9's**.

Unit 9 (make 80)

12. Sew 2 **Unit 7's**, 1 **Unit 8**, and 1 **Unit 9** together to make **Unit 10**. Make 80 **Unit 10's**.

Unit 10 (make 80)

13. Sew 4 **Unit 10's** together to make **Block**. Make 20 **Blocks**.

Block (make 20)

MAKING THE MIDDLE BORDER

*Use ¼" seam allowances throughout. The colors form diagonal lines that repeat around the entire quilt. Refer to **Quilt Top Diagram**, page 24, and pay special attention to color placement while constructing the **Middle Border**.*

1. Sew 4 tan **strips,** 1 red **strip,** 1 blue **strip**, 1 green **strip**, and 1 brown **strip** together to make **Strip Set D**. Make 5 **Strip Set D's**. Cut across **Strip Set D's** at 1½" intervals to make **Unit 11**. Make 42 **Unit 11's**.

Strip Set D (make 5)   **Unit 11** (make 42)

1½"

2. Sew 4 tan **strips,** 1 red **strip,** 1 blue **strip,** 1 green **strip,** and 1 brown **strip** together to make **Strip Set E**. Make 5 **Strip Set E's**. Cut across **Strip Set E's** at 1¹/₂" intervals to make **Unit 12**. Make 42 **Unit 12's**.

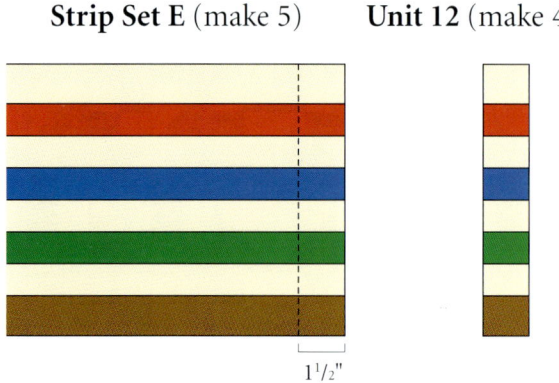

3. Sew 4 tan **strips,** 1 brown **strip,** 1 red **strip,** 1 blue **strip,** and 1 green **strip** together to make **Strip Set F**. Make 5 **Strip Set F's**. Cut across **Strip Set F's** at 1¹/₂" intervals to make **Unit 13**. Make 42 **Unit 13's**.

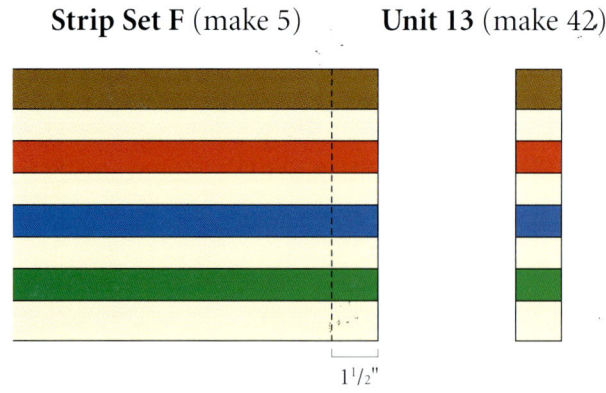

4. Sew 4 tan **strips,** 1 brown **strip,** 1 red **strip,** 1 blue **strip,** and 1 green **strip** together to make **Strip Set G**. Make 5 **Strip Set G's**. Cut across **Strip Set G's** at 1¹/₂" intervals to make **Unit 14**. Make 42 **Unit 14's**.

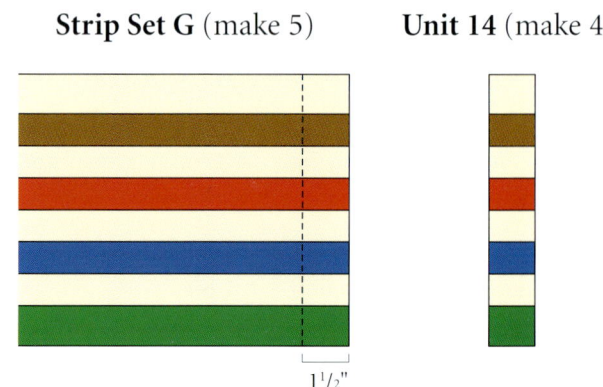

5. Sew 1 **Unit 11**, 1 **Unit 12**, 1 **Unit 13**, and 1 **Unit 14** together to make **Unit 15**. Make 21 **Unit 15's**.

Unit 15 (make 21)

6. Sew 1 **Unit 14**, 1 **Unit 13**, 1 **Unit 12**, and 1 **Unit 11** together to make **Unit 16**. Make 19 **Unit 16's**.

Unit 16 (make 19)

7. Remove seam at center of remaining **Unit 11's**, **Unit 12's**, **Unit 13's**, and **Unit 14's**. Sew resulting units together to make 2 **Unit 17's** and 2 **Unit 18's**.

Unit 17 (make 2)

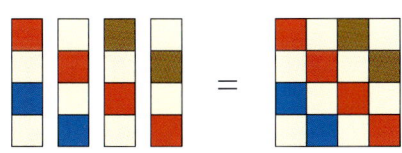

Unit 18 (make 2)

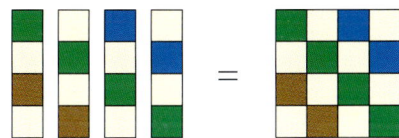

8. Sew 11 **Unit 15's** together end to end to make **left side middle border**.
9. Sew 10 **Unit 15's** together end to end; sew 1 **Unit 17** to one end and 1 **Unit 18** to the other end to make **right side middle border**.
10. Sew 10 **Unit 16's** together end to end to make **top middle border**.
11. Sew 9 **Unit 16's** together end to end; sew 1 **Unit 17** to one end and 1 **Unit 18** to the other end to make **bottom middle border**.

ASSEMBLING THE QUILT TOP

*Use $1/4$" seam allowances throughout. For all borders, match centers and corners and ease in any fullness. Refer to **Quilt Top Diagram**, page 24, and photo, page 25, for placement.*

1. Sew 4 **Blocks** together to make **Row**. Make 5 **Rows**.
2. Sew **Rows** together to complete center section of quilt top.
3. Add **side**, **top**, then **bottom inner borders** to quilt top. Repeat to add **middle** and **outer borders**.

COMPLETING THE QUILT

1. Follow **Quilting**, page 36, to mark, layer, and quilt as desired. Our quilt is machine quilted.
2. Cut a 33" square for binding. Follow **Binding**, page 40, to bind quilt using $2^1/2$"w bias binding with mitered corners.

Quilt Top Diagram

MY LITTLE Fat Quarter Quilt

Quilt made by Velda Grubbs and Dianna Olson.

Quilt Size: 55" x 71" (140 cm x 180 cm)
Block Size: 16" x 16" (41 cm x 41 cm)

YARDAGE REQUIREMENTS

Fat quarters measure approximately 18" x 22" (46 cm x 56 cm). The number of fat quarters we recommend is generous to allow for more variety in prints. Yardages are based on 43"/44" (109 cm/112 cm) wide fabric.

- 11 fat quarters of assorted cream print fabrics
- 5 fat quarters of assorted green print fabrics
- 4 fat quarters of assorted aqua print fabrics
- 3 fat quarters of assorted pink print fabrics
- 3 fat quarters of assorted purple print fabrics
- 2 yds (1.8 m) of cream print fabric for borders
- 4 1/2 yds (4.1 m) of fabric for backing
- 7/8 yd (80 cm) of fabric for binding

You will also need:
- 63" x 79" (160 cm x 201 cm) piece of batting

CUTTING OUT THE PIECES

*Measurements include 1/4" seam allowances. Cutting lengths given for borders are exact. Follow **Rotary Cutting**, page 34, to cut fabric. Cut strips from fat quarters across 18" length.*

From assorted cream print fabrics:
- Cut 20 strips 2 7/8"w. From these strips, cut 96 **squares** 2 7/8" x 2 7/8".
- Cut 88 **strips** 1 1/2"w.

From assorted green print fabrics:
- Cut 20 strips 2 7/8"w. From these strips, cut 96 **squares** 2 7/8" x 2 7/8".
- Cut 12 **strips** 1 1/2"w.

From assorted aqua print fabrics:
- Cut 32 **strips** 1 1/2"w.

From assorted pink print fabrics:
- Cut 22 **strips** 1 1/2"w.

From assorted purple print fabrics:
- Cut 22 **strips** 1 1/2"w.

From cream print fabric for borders:
- Cut 2 *lengthwise* **side outer borders** 3 1/2" x 64 1/2".
- Cut 2 *lengthwise* **top/bottom outer borders** 3 1/2" x 54 1/2".
- Cut 2 *lengthwise* **side inner borders** 4 1/2" x 48 1/2".
- Cut 2 *lengthwise* **top/bottom inner borders** 4 1/2" x 40 1/2".

MAKING THE BLOCKS

*Use 1/4" seam allowances throughout. Follow **Piecing**, page 35, and **Pressing**, page 36, to make **Blocks**.*

1. Draw diagonal line (corner to corner) on wrong side of each cream **square**. With right sides together, place 1 cream **square** on top of 1 green **square**. Stitch seam 1/4" from each side of drawn line (**Fig. 1**).

Fig. 1

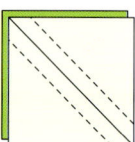

2. Cut along drawn line and press open to make 2 **Triangle-Squares**. Make 192 **Triangle-Squares**.

Triangle-Squares (make 192)

3. Sew 1 aqua **strip** and 1 cream **strip** together to make **Strip Set A**. Make 20 **Strip Set A's**. Cut across **Strip Set A's** at 1¹⁄₂" intervals to make **Unit 1**. Make 192 **Unit 1's**.

Strip Set A (make 20)   **Unit 1** (make 192)

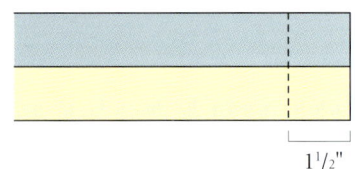 

4. Sew 1 pink **strip** and 1 cream **strip** together to make **Strip Set B**. Make 10 **Strip Set B's**. Cut across **Strip Set B's** at 1¹⁄₂" intervals to make **Unit 2**. Make 96 **Unit 2's**.

Strip Set B (make 10)   **Unit 2** (make 96)

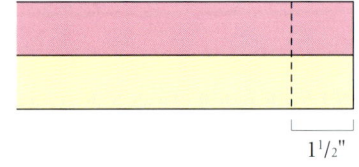 

5. Sew 1 purple **strip** and 1 cream **strip** together to make **Strip Set C**. Make 10 **Strip Set C's**. Cut across **Strip Set C's** at 1¹⁄₂" intervals to make **Unit 3**. Make 96 **Unit 3's**.

Strip Set C (make 10)   **Unit 3** (make 96)

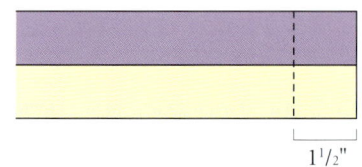 

6. Sew 2 **Unit 1's** together to make **Unit 4**. Make 96 **Unit 4's**.

Unit 4 (make 96)

7. Sew 2 **Unit 2's** together to make **Unit 5**. Make 48 **Unit 5's**.

Unit 5 (make 48)

8. Sew 2 **Unit 3's** together to make **Unit 6**. Make 48 **Unit 6's**.

Unit 6 (make 48)

9. Sew 2 **Unit 4's** and 2 **Triangle-Squares** together to make **Unit 7**. Make 48 **Unit 7's**.

Unit 7 (make 48)

10. Sew 2 **Unit 5's** and 2 **Triangle-Squares** together to make **Unit 8**. Make 24 **Unit 8's**.

Unit 8 (make 24)

11. Sew 2 **Unit 6's** and 2 **Triangle-Squares** together to make **Unit 9**. Make 24 **Unit 9's**.

Unit 9 (make 24)

12. Sew 2 **Unit 7's**, 1 **Unit 8**, and 1 **Unit 9** together to make **Unit 10**. Make 24 **Unit 10's**.

Unit 10 (make 24)

13. Sew 4 **Unit 10's** together to make **Block**. Make 6 **Blocks**.

Block (make 6)

29

MAKING THE MIDDLE BORDER

*Use ¹/₄" seam allowances throughout. The colors form diagonal lines that repeat around the entire quilt. Refer to **Quilt Top Diagram**, page 32, and pay special attention to color placement while constructing the **Middle Border**.*

1. Sew 4 cream **strips,** 1 pink **strip,** 1 purple **strip,** 1 aqua **strip,** and 1 green **strip** together to make **Strip Set D**. Make 3 **Strip Set D's**. Cut across **Strip Set D's** at 1¹/₂" intervals to make **Unit 11**. Make 26 **Unit 11's**.

   Strip Set D (make 3)   **Unit 11** (make 26)

   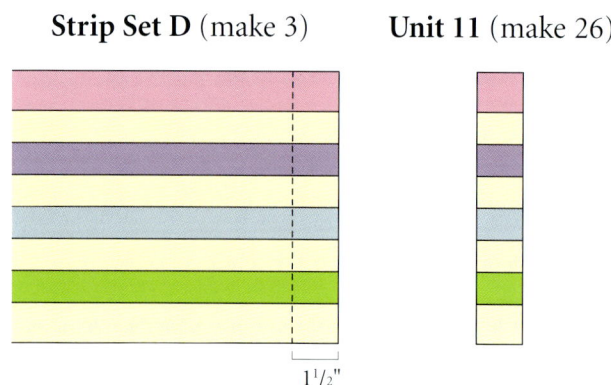

2. Sew 4 cream **strips,** 1 pink **strip,** 1 purple **strip,** 1 aqua **strip,** and 1 green **strip** together to make **Strip Set E**. Make 3 **Strip Set E's**. Cut across **Strip Set E's** at 1¹/₂" intervals to make **Unit 12**. Make 26 **Unit 12's**.

   Strip Set E (make 3)   **Unit 12** (make 26)

   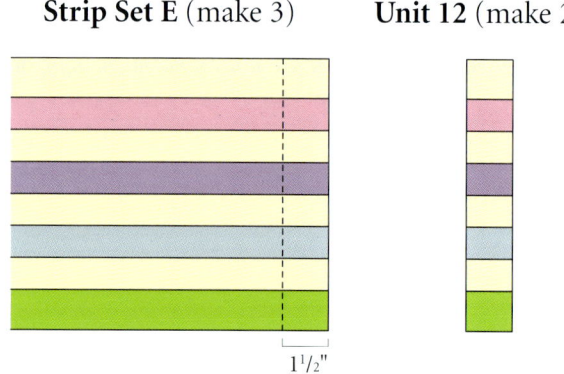

3. Sew 4 cream **strips,** 1 green **strip,** 1 pink **strip,** 1 purple **strip,** and 1 aqua **strip** together to make **Strip Set F**. Make 3 **Strip Set F's**. Cut across **Strip Set F's** at 1¹/₂" intervals to make **Unit 13**. Make 26 **Unit 13's**.

   Strip Set F (make 3)   **Unit 13** (make 26)

   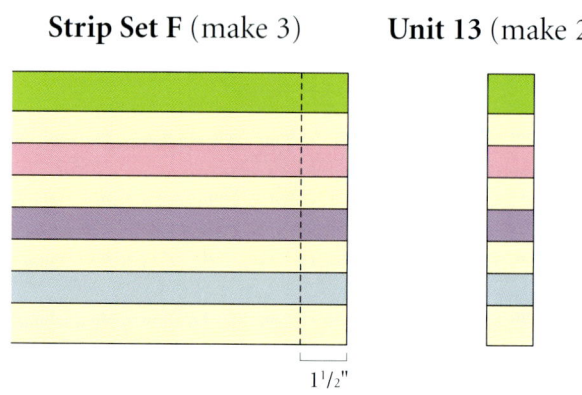

4. Sew 4 cream **strips,** 1 green **strip,** 1 pink **strip,** 1 purple **strip,** and 1 aqua **strip** together to make **Strip Set G**. Make 3 **Strip Set G's**. Cut across **Strip Set G's** at 1¹/₂" intervals to make **Unit 14**. Make 26 **Unit 14's**.

   Strip Set G (make 3)   **Unit 14** (make 26)

   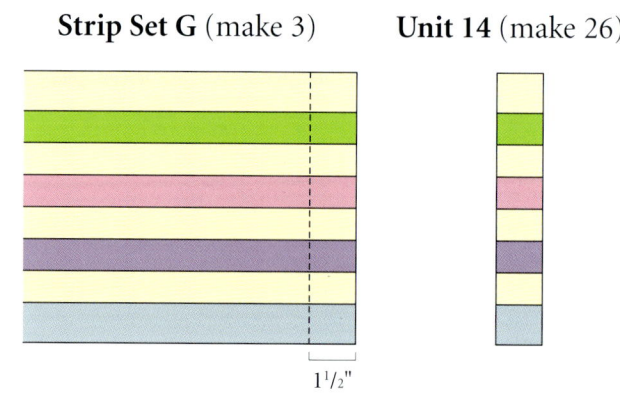

5. Sew 1 **Unit 11**, 1 **Unit 12**, 1 **Unit 13**, and 1 **Unit 14** together in the order shown to make **Unit 15**. Make 13 **Unit 15**'s.

Unit 15 (make 13)

6. Sew 1 **Unit 14**, 1 **Unit 13**, 1 **Unit 12**, and 1 **Unit 11** together in the order shown to make **Unit 16**. Make 11 **Unit 16**'s.

Unit 16 (make 11)

7. Remove seam at center of remaining **Unit 11**'s, **Unit 12**'s, **Unit 13**'s, and **Unit 14**'s. Sew resulting units together as shown to make 2 **Unit 17**'s and 2 **Unit 18**'s.

Unit 17 (make 2)

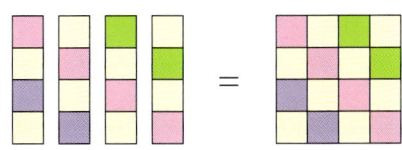

Unit 18 (make 2)

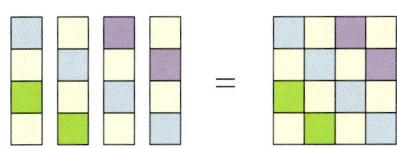

8. Sew 7 **Unit 15**'s together end to end to make **left side middle border**.
9. Sew 6 **Unit 15**'s together end to end; sew 1 **Unit 17** to one end and 1 **Unit 18** to the other end to make **right side middle border**.
10. Sew 6 **Unit 16**'s together end to end to make **top middle border**.
11. Sew 5 **Unit 16**'s together end to end; sew 1 **Unit 17** to one end and 1 **Unit 18** to the other end to make **bottom middle border**.

ASSEMBLING THE QUILT TOP

*Use ¹/₄" seam allowances throughout. For all borders, match centers and corners and ease in any fullness. Refer to **Quilt Top Diagram**, page 32, and photo, page 33, for placement.*

1. Sew 2 **Blocks** together to make **Row**. Make 3 **Rows**.
2. Sew **Rows** together to complete center section of quilt top.
3. Add **side**, **top**, then **bottom inner borders** to quilt top. Repeat to add **middle** and **outer borders**.

COMPLETING THE QUILT

1. Follow **Quilting**, page 36, to mark, layer, and quilt as desired. Our quilt is machine quilted.
2. Cut a 27" square for binding. Follow **Binding**, page 40, to bind quilt using 2$\frac{1}{2}$"w bias binding with mitered corners.

Quilt Top Diagram

32

GENERAL INSTRUCTIONS

To make your quilting easier and more enjoyable, we encourage you to carefully read all of the general instructions, study the color photographs, and familiarize yourself with the individual project instructions before beginning a project.

FABRICS

SELECTING FABRICS

Choose high-quality, medium-weight 100% cotton fabrics. All-cotton fabrics hold a crease better, fray less, and are easier to quilt than cotton/polyester blends.

Yardage requirements listed for each project are based on 43"/44" (109 cm/112 cm) wide fabric with a "usable" width of 40" after shrinkage and trimming selvages. Actual usable width will probably vary slightly from fabric to fabric. Our recommended yardage lengths should be adequate for occasional re-squaring of fabric when many cuts are required.

"Fat quarters" are made by cutting one yard of fabric in half horizontally, then cutting resulting pieces in half vertically. Many fabric stores sell "fat quarters" individually, or in coordinating sets. "Fat quarters" measure approximately 18" x 22" (46 cm x 56 cm) and are used in two of our quilts ("My Big Fat Quarter Quilt" and "My Little Fat Quarter Quilt").

PREPARING FABRICS

We recommend that all fabrics be washed, dried, and pressed before cutting. If fabrics are not pre-washed, washing the finished quilt will cause shrinkage and give it a more "antiqued" look and feel. Bright and dark colors, which may run, should always be washed before cutting. After washing and drying fabric, fold lengthwise with wrong sides together and matching selvages.

ROTARY CUTTING

Rotary cutting has brought speed and accuracy to quiltmaking by allowing quilters to easily cut strips of fabric and then cut those strips into smaller pieces.

- Place fabric on work surface with fold closest to you.

- Cut all strips from the selvage-to-selvage width of the fabric unless otherwise indicated in project instructions.

- Square left edge of fabric using rotary cutter and rulers (**Figs. 1 - 2**).

Fig. 1

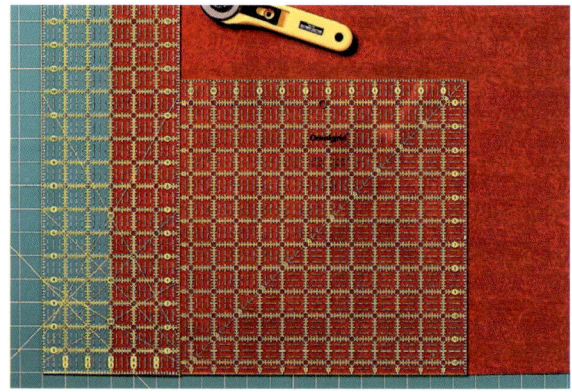

Fig. 2

- To cut each strip required for a project, place ruler over cut edge of fabric, aligning desired marking on ruler with cut edge; make cut (**Fig. 3**).

Fig. 3

- When cutting several strips from a single piece of fabric, it is important to make sure that cuts remain at a perfect right angle to the fold; re-square fabric as needed.

TEMPLATE CUTTING

Our piecing template patterns have two lines – a solid cutting line and a dashed line showing the $1/4$" seam allowance.

1. To make a template from a pattern, use a permanent fine-point pen and a ruler to carefully trace pattern onto template plastic, making sure to transfer any alignment and grain line markings. Cut out template along inner edge of drawn line. Check template against original pattern for accuracy.
2. Place template face down on wrong side of fabric, aligning grain line on template with straight grain of fabric. Use a sharp fabric-marking pencil to draw around template. Transfer all alignment markings to fabric. Cut out fabric piece using scissors or rotary cutting equipment.

PIECING

Precise cutting, followed by accurate piecing, will ensure that all pieces of quilt top fit together well.

HAND PIECING

- Use ruler and sharp fabric marking pencil to draw all seam lines and transfer any alignment markings onto back of cut pieces.
- Matching right sides, pin two pieces together, using pins to mark corners.
- Use Running Stitch to sew pieces together along drawn line, backstitching at beginning and end of seam.
- Do not extend stitches into seam allowances.
- Run 5 or 6 stitches onto needle before pulling needle through fabric.
- To add stability, backstitch every $3/4$" to 1".

MACHINE PIECING

- Set sewing machine stitch length for approximately 11 stitches per inch.
- Use neutral-colored general-purpose sewing thread (not quilting thread) in needle and in bobbin.
- An accurate $1/4$" seam allowance is *essential*. Presser feet that are $1/4$" wide are available for most sewing machines.
- When piecing, always place pieces right sides together and match raw edges; pin if necessary.
- Chain piecing saves time and will usually result in more accurate piecing.
- Trim away points of seam allowances that extend beyond edges of sewn pieces.

Sewing Strip Sets

When there are several strips to assemble into a strip set, first sew strips together into pairs, then sew pairs together to form strip set. To help avoid distortion, sew seams in opposite directions (**Fig. 4**).

Fig. 4

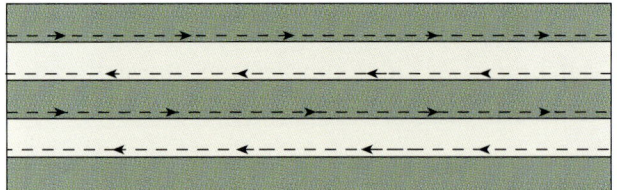

Sewing Across Seam Intersections

When sewing across intersection of two seams, place pieces right sides together and match seams exactly, making sure seam allowances are pressed in opposite directions (**Fig. 5**).

Fig. 5

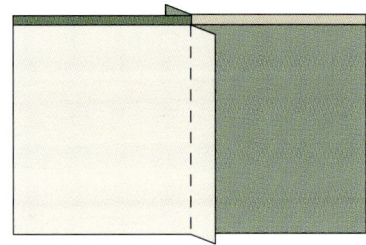

Sewing Sharp Points

To ensure sharp points when joining triangular or diagonal pieces, stitch across the center of the "X" (shown in pink) formed on wrong side by previous seams (**Fig. 6**).

Fig. 6

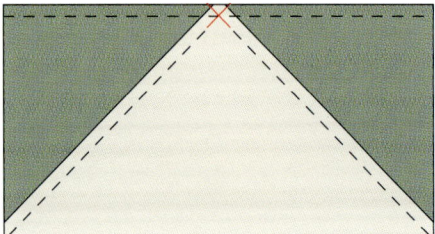

PRESSING

- Use steam iron set on "Cotton" for all pressing.

- Press after sewing each seam.

- Seam allowances are almost always pressed to one side, usually toward darker fabric. However, to reduce bulk it may occasionally be necessary to press seam allowances toward the lighter fabric or even to press them open.

- To prevent a dark fabric seam allowance from showing through a light fabric, trim darker seam allowance slightly narrower than lighter seam allowance.

- To press long seams, such as those in long strip sets, without curving or other distortion, lay strips across width of the ironing board.

QUILTING

Quilting holds the three layers (top, batting, and backing) of the quilt together and can be done by hand or machine. Because marking, layering, and quilting are interrelated and may be done in different orders depending on circumstances, please read entire **Quilting** *section, pages 36 - 40, before beginning project.*

TYPES OF QUILTING DESIGNS

In the Ditch Quilting

Quilting along seam lines or along edges of appliquéd pieces is called "in the ditch" quilting. This type of quilting should be done on side **opposite** seam allowance and does not have to be marked.

Outline Quilting

Quilting a consistent distance, usually $1/4$", from seam or appliqué is called "outline" quilting. Outline quilting may be marked, or $1/4$" masking tape may be placed along seam lines for quilting guide. (Do not leave tape on quilt longer than necessary, since it may leave an adhesive residue.)

Motif Quilting
Quilting a design, such as a feathered wreath, is called "motif" quilting. This type of quilting should be marked before basting quilt layers together.

Echo Quilting
Quilting that follows the outline of an appliquéd or pieced design with two or more parallel lines is called "echo" quilting. This type of quilting may be marked or stitched using a guide.

Channel Quilting
Quilting with straight, parallel lines is called "channel" quilting. This type of quilting may be marked or stitched using a guide.

Crosshatch Quilting
Quilting straight lines in a grid pattern is called "crosshatch" quilting. Lines may be stitched parallel to edges of quilt or stitched diagonally. This type of quilting may be marked or stitched using a guide.

Meandering Quilting
Quilting in random curved lines and swirls is called "meandering" quilting. Quilting lines should not cross or touch each other. This type of quilting does not need to be marked.

Stipple Quilting
Meandering quilting that is very closely spaced is called "stipple" quilting. Stippling will flatten the area quilted and is often stitched in background areas to raise appliquéd or pieced designs. This type of quilting does not need to be marked.

MARKING QUILTING LINES
Quilting lines may be marked using fabric marking pencils, chalk markers, water- or air-soluble pens, or lead pencils.

Simple quilting designs may be marked with chalk or chalk pencil after basting. A small area may be marked, then quilted, before moving to next area to be marked. Intricate designs should be marked before basting using a more durable marker.

Caution: Some marks may be permanently set by pressing. **Test** different markers **on scrap fabric** to find one that marks clearly and can be thoroughly removed.

A wide variety of pre-cut quilting stencils, as well as entire books of quilting patterns, are available. Using a stencil makes it easier to mark intricate or repetitive designs.

To make a stencil from a pattern, center template plastic over pattern and use a permanent marker to trace pattern onto plastic. Use a craft knife with single or double blade to cut channels along traced lines (**Fig. 7**).

Fig. 7

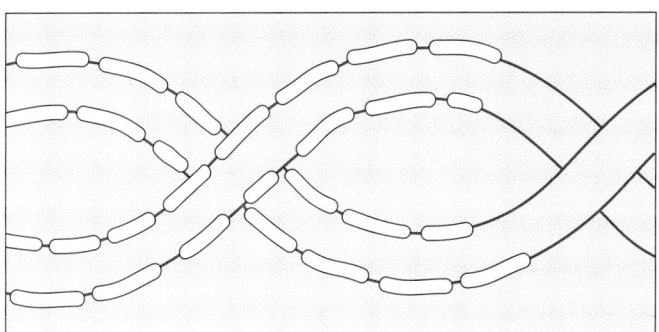

PREPARING THE BACKING

To allow for slight shifting of quilt top during quilting, backing should be approximately 4" larger on all sides. Yardage requirements listed for quilt backings are calculated for 43"/44"w fabric. Using 90"w or 108"w fabric for the backing of a bed-sized quilt may eliminate piecing. To piece a backing using 43"/44"w fabric, use the following instructions.

1. Measure length and width of quilt top; add 8" to each measurement.
2. If determined width is less than 80", cut backing fabric into two lengths slightly longer than determined **length** measurement. Trim selvages. Place lengths with right sides facing and sew long edges together, forming a tube (**Fig. 8**). Match seams and press along one fold (**Fig. 9**). Cut along pressed fold to form single piece (**Fig. 10**).

Fig. 8   **Fig. 9** 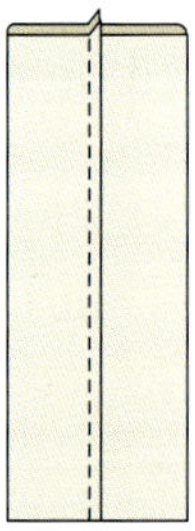   **Fig. 10**

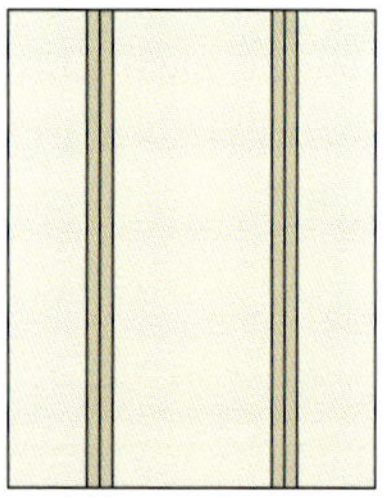

3. If determined width is 80" or more, cut backing fabric into three lengths slightly longer than determined **width** measurement. Trim selvages. Sew long edges together to form single piece.
4. Trim backing to size determined in Step 1; press seam allowances open.

CHOOSING THE BATTING

The appropriate batting will make quilting easier. For fine hand quilting, choose low-loft batting. All cotton or cotton/polyester blend battings work well for machine quilting because the cotton helps "grip" quilt layers. If quilt is to be tied, a high-loft batting, sometimes called extra-loft or fat batting, may be used to make quilt "fluffy."

Types of batting include cotton, polyester, wool, cotton/polyester blend, cotton/wool blend, and silk.

When selecting batting, refer to package labels for characteristics and care instructions. Cut batting the size indicated in project instructions.

ASSEMBLING THE QUILT

1. Examine wrong side of quilt top closely; trim any seam allowances and clip any threads that may show through front of the quilt. Press quilt top, being careful not to "set" any marked quilting lines.
2. Place backing **wrong** side up on flat surface. Use masking tape to tape edges of backing to surface. Place batting on top of backing fabric. Smooth batting gently, being careful not to stretch or tear. Center quilt top **right** side up on batting.
3. If hand quilting, begin in center and work toward outer edges to hand baste all layers together. Use long stitches and place basting lines approximately 4" apart (**Fig. 11**). Smooth fullness or wrinkles toward outer edges.

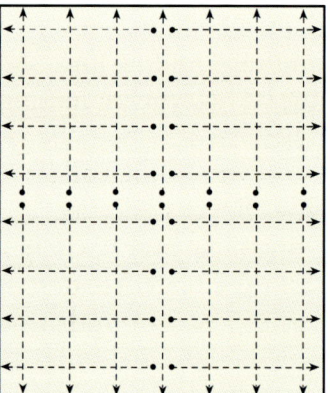

Fig. 11

4. If machine quilting, use 1" rustproof safety pins to "pin-baste" all layers together, spacing pins approximately 4" apart. Begin at center and work toward outer edges to secure all layers. If possible, place pins away from areas that will be quilted, although pins may be removed as needed when quilting.

HAND QUILTING

The quilting stitch is a basic running stitch that forms a broken line on quilt top and backing. Stitches on quilt top and backing should be straight and equal in length.

1. Secure center of quilt in hoop or frame. Check quilt top and backing to make sure they are smooth. To help prevent puckers, always begin quilting in the center of quilt and work toward outside edges.
2. Thread needle with 18" - 20" length of quilting thread; knot one end. Using thimble, insert needle into quilt top and batting approximately 1/2" from quilting line. Bring needle up on quilting line (**Fig. 12**); when knot catches on quilt top, give thread a quick, short pull to "pop" knot through fabric into batting (**Fig. 13**).

Fig. 12   **Fig. 13**

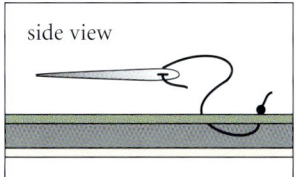
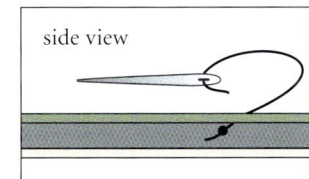

3. Holding needle with sewing hand and placing other hand underneath quilt, use thimble to push tip of needle down through all layers. As soon as needle touches finger underneath, use that finger to push tip of needle only back up through layers to top of quilt. (The amount of needle showing above fabric determines length of quilting stitch.) Referring to **Fig. 14**, rock needle up and down, taking 3 - 6 stitches before bringing needle and thread completely through layers. Check back of quilt to make sure stitches are going through all layers. If necessary, make one stitch at a time when quilting through seam allowances or along curves and corners.

Fig. 14

4. At end of thread, knot thread close to fabric and "pop" knot into batting; clip thread close to fabric.
5. Move hoop as often as necessary. Thread may be left dangling and picked up again after returning to that part of quilt.

MACHINE QUILTING METHODS

Use general-purpose thread in bobbin. Do not use quilting thread. Thread the needle of machine with general-purpose thread or transparent monofilament thread to make quilting blend with quilt top fabrics. Use decorative thread, such as a metallic or contrasting-color general-purpose thread, to make quilting lines stand out more.

Straight Line Quilting

The term "straight-line" is somewhat deceptive, since curves (especially gentle ones) as well as straight lines can be stitched with this technique.

1. Set stitch length for 6 - 10 stitches per inch and attach walking foot to sewing machine.
2. Determine which section of quilt will have longest continuous quilting line, oftentimes area from center top to center bottom. Roll up and secure each edge of quilt to help reduce the bulk, keeping fabrics smooth. Smaller projects may not need to be rolled.

3. Begin stitching on longest quilting line, using very short stitches for the first ¹⁄₄" to "lock" quilting. Stitch across project, using one hand on each side of walking foot to slightly spread fabric and to guide fabric through machine. Lock stitches at end of quilting line.
4. Continue machine quilting, stitching longer quilting lines first to stabilize quilt before moving on to other areas.

Free Motion Quilting
Free motion quilting may be free form or may follow a marked pattern.
1. Attach darning foot to sewing machine and lower or cover feed dogs.
2. Position quilt under darning foot; lower foot. Holding top thread, take one stitch and pull bobbin thread to top of quilt. To "lock" beginning of quilting line, hold top and bobbin threads while making 3 to 5 stitches in place.
3. Use one hand on each side of darning foot to slightly spread fabric and to move fabric through the machine. Even stitch length is achieved by using smooth, flowing hand motion and steady machine speed. Slow machine speed and fast hand movement will create long stitches. Fast machine speed and slow hand movement will create short stitches. Move quilt sideways, back and forth, in a circular motion, or in a random motion to create desired designs; do not rotate quilt. Lock stitches at end of each quilting line.

MAKING A HANGING SLEEVE
Attaching a hanging sleeve to back of wall hanging or quilt before the binding is added allows project to be displayed on wall.
1. Measure width of quilt top edge and subtract 1". Cut piece of fabric 7"w by determined measurement, piecing as necessary.
2. Press short edges of fabric piece ¹⁄₄" to wrong side; press edges ¹⁄₄" to wrong side again and machine stitch in place.
3. Matching wrong sides, fold piece in half lengthwise to form tube.
4. Follow project instructions to sew binding to quilt top and to trim backing and batting. Before blindstitching binding to backing, match raw edges and stitch hanging sleeve to center top edge on back of quilt.

5. Finish binding quilt, treating hanging sleeve as part of backing.
6. Blindstitch bottom of hanging sleeve to backing, taking care not to stitch through to front of quilt.

BINDING
Binding encloses the raw edges of quilt. Because of its stretchiness, bias binding works well for binding projects with curves or rounded corners and tends to lie smooth and flat in any given circumstance. Binding may also be cut from straight lengthwise or crosswise grain of fabric.

MAKING CONTINUOUS BIAS STRIP BINDING
Bias strips for binding can simply be cut and pieced to desired length. However, when a long length of binding is needed, the "continuous" method is quick and accurate.
1. Cut square from binding fabric the size indicated in project instructions. Cut square in half diagonally to make two triangles.
2. With right sides together and using ¹⁄₄" seam allowance, sew triangles together (**Fig. 15**); press seam allowances open.

Fig. 15

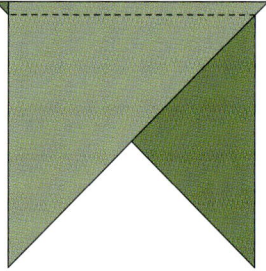

3. On wrong side of fabric, draw lines the width of binding as specified in project instructions, usually 2¹⁄₂" (**Fig. 16**). Cut off any remaining fabric less than this width.

Fig. 16

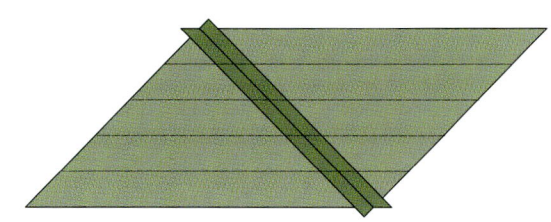

4. With right sides inside, bring short edges together to form tube; match raw edges so that first drawn line of top section meets second drawn line of bottom section (**Fig. 17**).

Fig. 17

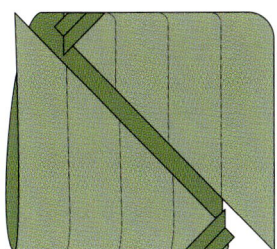

5. Carefully pin edges together by inserting pins through drawn lines at point where drawn lines intersect, making sure pins go through intersections on both sides. Using $1/4$" seam allowance, sew edges together; press seam allowances open.
6. To cut continuous strip, begin cutting along first drawn line (**Fig. 18**). Continue cutting along drawn line around tube.

Fig. 18

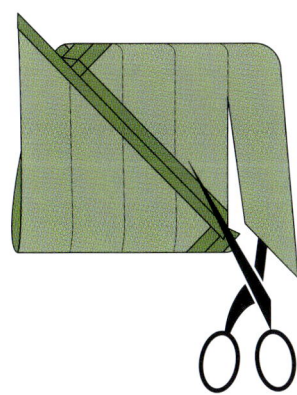

7. Trim ends of bias strip square.
8. Matching wrong sides and raw edges, carefully press bias strip in half lengthwise to complete binding.

ATTACHING BINDING WITH MITERED CORNERS

1. Beginning with one end near center on bottom edge of quilt, lay binding around quilt to make sure that seams in binding will not end up at a corner. Adjust placement if necessary. Matching raw edges of binding to raw edge of quilt top, pin binding to right side of quilt along one edge.
2. When you reach first corner, mark $1/4$" from corner of quilt top (**Fig. 19**).

Fig. 19

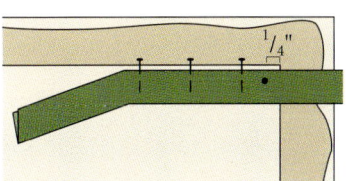

3. Beginning approximately 10" from end of binding and using a $1/4$" seam allowance, sew binding to quilt, backstitching at beginning of stitching and at mark (**Fig. 20**). Lift needle out of fabric and clip thread.

Fig. 20

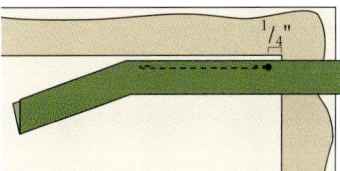

4. Fold binding as shown in **Figs. 21 – 22** and pin binding to adjacent side, matching raw edges. When you've reached the next corner, mark $1/4$" from edge of quilt.

Fig. 21   **Fig. 22**

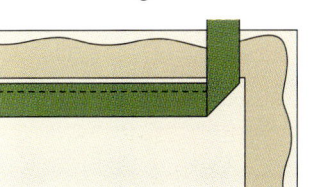 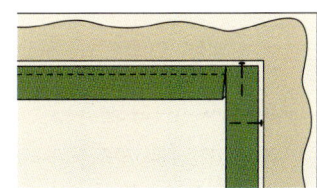

5. Backstitching at edge of quilt top, sew pinned binding to quilt (**Fig. 23**); backstitch at the next mark. Lift needle out of fabric and clip thread.

Fig. 23

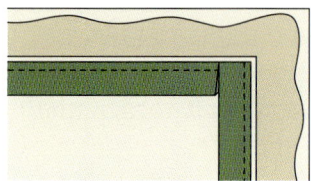

6. Continue sewing binding to quilt, stopping approximately 10" from starting point (**Fig. 24**).

Fig. 24

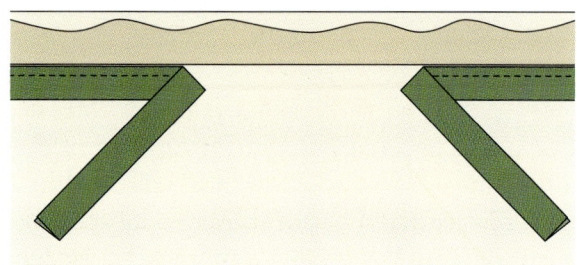

7. Bring beginning and end of binding to center of opening and fold each end back, leaving a ¼" space between folds (**Fig. 25**). Finger-press folds.

Fig. 25

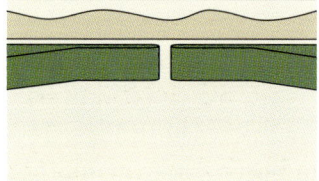

8. Unfold ends of binding and draw a line across wrong side in finger-pressed crease. Draw a line through the lengthwise pressed fold of binding at same spot to create a cross mark. With edge of ruler at marked cross, line up 45° angle marking on ruler with one long side of binding. Draw a diagonal line from edge to edge. Repeat on remaining end, making sure that the two diagonal lines are angled the same way (**Fig. 26**).

Fig. 26

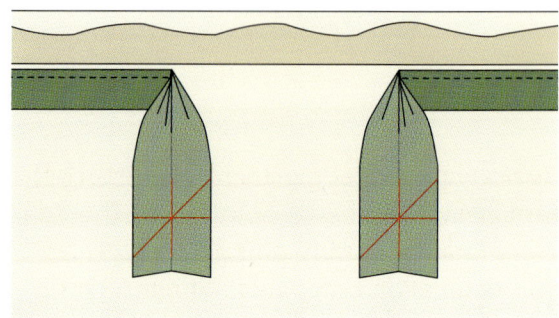

9. Matching right sides and diagonal lines, pin binding ends together at right angles (**Fig. 27**).

Fig. 27

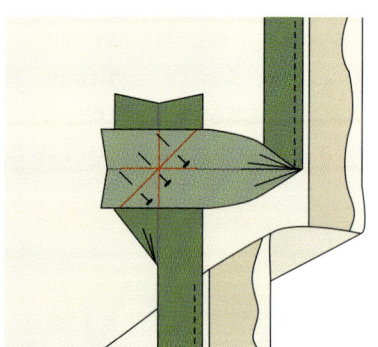

0. Machine stitch along diagonal line (**Fig. 28**), removing pins as you stitch.

Fig. 28

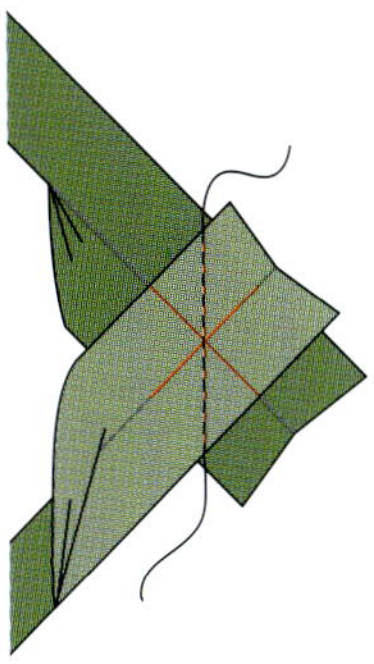

1. Lay binding against quilt to double check that it is correct length.
2. Trim binding ends, leaving a ¼" seam allowance; press seam allowances open. Stitch binding to quilt.
3. If using 2½"w binding (finished size ½"), trim backing and batting a scant ¼" larger than quilt top so that batting and backing will fill the binding when it is folded over to quilt backing.
4. On one edge of quilt, fold binding over to quilt backing and pin pressed edge in place, covering stitching line (**Fig. 29**). On adjacent side, fold binding over, forming a mitered corner (**Fig. 30**). Repeat to pin remainder of binding in place.

Fig. 29   **Fig. 30**

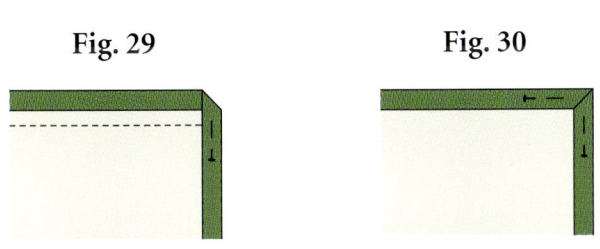

15. Blindstitch binding to backing, taking care not to stitch through to front of quilt (**Fig. 31**).

Fig. 31

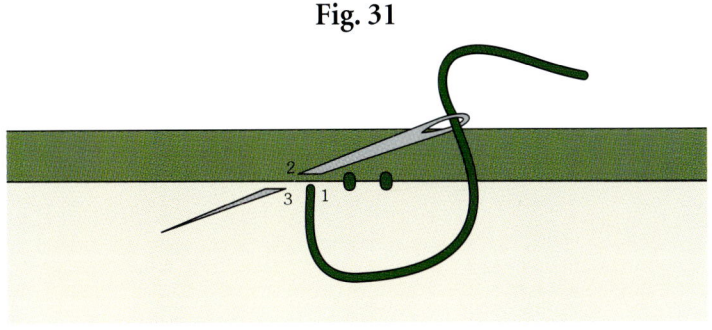

SIGNING AND DATING YOUR QUILT

A completed quilt is a work of art and should be signed and dated. There are many different ways to do this and numerous books on the subject. The label should reflect the style of the quilt, the occasion or person for which it was made, and the quilter's own particular talents. Following are suggestions for recording the history of the quilt or adding a sentiment for future generations.

- Embroider quilter's name, date, and any additional information on the quilt top or backing. Matching floss, such as cream floss on white border, will leave a subtle record. Bright or contrasting floss will make the information stand out.

- Make a label from muslin and use a permanent marker to write information. Use different colored permanent markers to make label more decorative. Stitch label to back of quilt.

- Use photo-transfer paper to add image to white or cream fabric label. Stitch label to back of quilt.

- Piece an extra block from the quilt top pattern to use as a label. Add information with permanent fabric pen. Appliqué block to back of quilt.

Metric Conversion Chart

Inches x 2.54 = centimeters (cm)	Yards x .9144 = meters (m)
Inches x 25.4 = millimeters (mm)	Yards x 91.44 = centimeters (cm)
Inches x .0254 = meters (m)	Centimeters x .3937 = inches (")
	Meters x 1.0936 = yards (yd)

Standard Equivalents

1/8"	3.2 mm	0.32 cm	1/8 yard	11.43 cm	0.11 m
1/4"	6.35 mm	0.635 cm	1/4 yard	22.86 cm	0.23 m
3/8"	9.5 mm	0.95 cm	3/8 yard	34.29 cm	0.34 m
1/2"	12.7 mm	1.27 cm	1/2 yard	45.72 cm	0.46 m
5/8"	15.9 mm	1.59 cm	5/8 yard	57.15 cm	0.57 m
3/4"	19.1 mm	1.91 cm	3/4 yard	68.58 cm	0.69 m
7/8"	22.2 mm	2.22 cm	7/8 yard	80 cm	0.8 m
1"	25.4 mm	2.54 cm	1 yard	91.44 cm	0.91 m

Machine quilting by The Quilter's Loft of DeKalb, IL, 1-815-787-3377.

©2004 by Leisure Arts, Inc., 5701 Ranch Drive, Little Rock, AR 72223. All rights reserved. This publication is protected under federal copyright laws. Reproduction or distribution of this publication or any other Leisure Arts publication, including publications which are out of print, is prohibited unless specifically authorized. This includes, but is not limited to, any form of reproduction or distribution on or through the Internet, including posting, scanning, or e-mail transmission.

We have made every effort to ensure that these instructions are accurate and complete. We cannot, however, be responsible for human error, typographical mistakes, or variations in individual work.

Production Team: Technical Editor – Lisa Lancaster; Technical Writer – Frances Huddleston; Graphic Artist – Ashley Carozza; Photography Stylist – Cassie Newsome.